50

Reasons Why I Love You...

1

I love the way you

____.

2

I love your

____.

3

I love how you make me feel so

______________________.

4

I love our

________________________________.

5

I love when we

____.

6

I love to watch

with you.

7

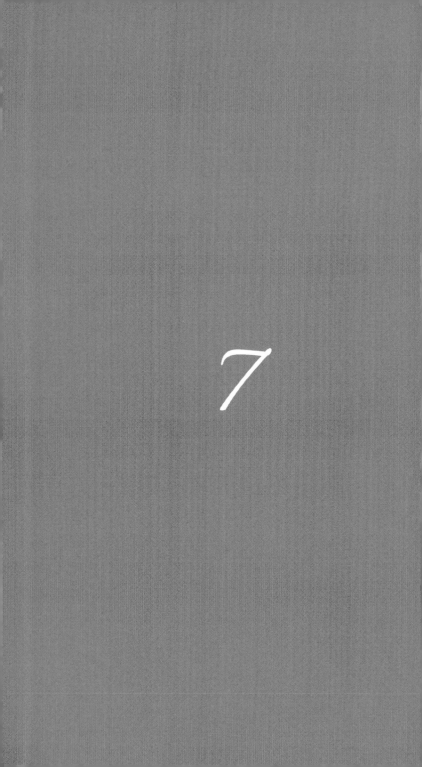

I love listening to

with you.

8

I love that you

_______________________________.

9

I love how you can make me

____

when you

____.

10

I love watching you when

____.

11

I love that I get to call you

______________________________.

12

I love eating

---

with you.

13

I love our trips to

____.

14

I would love to travel to

and

with you.

15

I love how you don't

____.

16

I love that you like to

____.

17

I would love to have

with you.

18

I love how you say

____.

19

I love that you're a

person.

20

I miss your

when you're not with me.

21

I would love to

with you.

22

I love to see you wear

______________________________.

23

I love you to the

& back!

24

I love how we are awesome at

______________________________.

25

I love to play

with you.

26

If we were animals.. then I would be a

____

and you would be a

____.

27

I love the first time I saw you

28

I love the

that we share.

29

I love when you gave me

____.

30

I would love to build

with you.

31

I love it so much when you

____

So please dont stop

____.

32

You are incredible at

____.

33

You make me want to be a better

_______________________________.

34

Your

is out of this world.

35

I love to

on our days off.

36

My dream date with you is to

____

and

______________________________.

37

You make me laugh so hard when

____.

38

Your

is so adorable.

39

I wish I could

like you.

40

You caught my eye by

---

when we first met.

41

You still give me butterflies when you

____.

42

I love how we always

______________________________.

43

I love knowing that

____.

44

Don't change the way you

____.

45

Your love makes me

46

I love dreaming about

with you.

47

I would fly to

with you tonight.

48

We need to

again.

49

The best advice you gave me was

____.

50

I love you,

______________________________.

61216686R00058

Made in the USA
Lexington, KY
03 March 2017